Bhagav: ____

~

The Perfect Philosophy

15 Reasons That Make the Song of God the Most Scientific Ideology

HARI CHETAN

A Gift for You

In the daily commotion that characterizes our lives nowadays, it is quite easy to lose track of oneself. And so it is important for us to maintain our mental equilibrium by connecting with our spiritual selves on a regular basis.

Download Hari Chetan's **free Bhagavad Gita Workbook** designed especially for the readers of his books.

This workbook will help you test your knowledge of the core concepts given in the Bhagavad Gita, and to keep you on track in your spiritual journey.

Try it. It's free to download and is very useful!

Visit **www.harichetan.com** to download.

Thoughts of Intellectuals on the Bhagavad Gita

"When doubts haunt me, when disappointments stare me in the face, and I see not one ray of hope on the horizon, I turn to Bhagavad Gita and find a verse to comfort me; and I immediately begin to smile in the midst of overwhelming sorrow. Those who meditate on the Gita will derive fresh joy and new meanings from it every day." ~ Mahatma Gandhi

"The marvel of the Bhagavad Gita is its truly beautiful revelation of life's wisdom which enables philosophy to blossom into religion." ~ Hermann Hesse

"(The Bhagavad Gita is) one of the most clear and comprehensive summaries of perennial philosophy ever revealed; hence its enduring value is subject not only to India but to all of humanity." ~ Aldous Huxley

"That the spiritual man need not be a recluse, that union with the divine life may be achieved and maintained in the midst of worldly affairs, that the obstacles to that union lie not outside us but within us — such is the central lesson of the Bhagavad Gita." ~ Annie Besant

"In the morning I bathe my intellect in the stupendous and cosmogonal philosophy of the Bhagavad Gita in comparison with which our modern world and its literature seem puny and trivial." ~ Henry David Thoreau

"I owed a magnificent day to the Bhagavad Gita. It was as if an empire spoke to us, nothing small or unworthy, but large, serene, consistent, the voice of an old intelligence which in another age and climate had pondered and thus disposed of the same questions which exercise us." ~ Ralph Waldo Emerson

"Bhagavad Gita is a true scripture of the human race, a living creation rather than a book, with a new message for every age and a new meaning for every civilization." ~ Sri Aurobindo

"The most beautiful, perhaps the only true philosophical song existing in any known tongue ... perhaps the deepest and loftiest thing the world has to show." ~ Wilhelm von Humboldt

"I am 90% through the Bhagavad Gita ... My inner Arjuna is being channelled." ~ Will Smith

"The Bhagavad Gita deals essentially with the spiritual foundation of human existence. It is a call of action to meet the obligations and duties of life; yet keeping in view the spiritual nature and grander purpose of the universe." ~ Jawaharlal Nehru

"I hesitate not to pronounce the Gita a performance of great originality, of sublimity of conception, reasoning and diction almost unequalled; and a single exception, amongst all the known religions of mankind." ~ Lord Warren Hastings

"Those are spiritual things to reflect upon yourself, life, the world around you and see things the other way. I thought it (the Bhagavad Gita) was quite appropriate." ~ Sunita Williams

The Bhagavad Gita Series

Book 1: Bhagavad Gita - The Perfect Philosophy: 15 Reasons That Make the Song of God the Most Scientific Ideology

Book 2: Bhagavad Gita (in English): The Authentic English Translation for Accurate and Unbiased Understanding

Book 3: 30 Days to Understanding the Bhagavad Gita: A Complete, Simple, and Step-by-Step Guide to the Million-Year-Old Confidential Knowledge

Book 4: The Bhagavad Gita Summarized and Simplified: A Comprehensive and Easy-to-Read Summary of the Divine Song of God

Book 5: Mind Management through the Bhagavad Gita: Master your Mindset in 21 Days and Discover Unlimited Happiness and Success

All Books: Bhagavad Gita (In English) – The Complete Collection: 5-Books-in-1

DEDICATED TO

All Spiritual Seekers

In Search of the Truth

"Thus, this most secret science has been told by Me to you, O Anagha; understanding this, one becomes wise and has his duties fulfilled, O descendant of Bharata."

[Lord Krishna to Arjuna - Bhagavad Gita 15.20]

Table of Contents

Introduction

I don't know you personally. So, I have no idea how old you are, what you do, and what experiences you've had in your life. But there is one thing I can confidently say about you:

If you have not read the Bhagavad Gita, you are missing out on one of life's greatest gifts.

I may have been a little hasty in stating that before offering a few warm greetings; but I prefer to get straight to the point. You see, life is short. Also, this book is meant to be a quick read.

Let me ask you a simple question: Assume that your life has a defined purpose, to fulfill which you have been sent to this world. You go through life doing everything right and appearing to be successful to yourself and others. But you never achieve that specific goal. Will your life then be considered a success even if you die with a trillion dollars in the bank?

This is the awareness that we need more than anything else today. And only true spirituality can provide us with such awareness.

We are a disoriented race today, hankering after trivial pleasures and uninterested in making an effort to learn about the important truths of life (and death).

Do we marvel at the transformation of sperm into a body with life? Does it look surprising to us when a caterpillar transforms into a lovely butterfly? Do we even care what gives a tiny seed the power to grow into a massive tree bearing fruits, flowers, and leaves?

Hardly!

We presume that these wonderful acts are caused by 'nature,' without bothering to ask, "Whose nature?"

We humans take pride in calling ourselves the most intelligent species on the planet. Although there is no doubt about us being the most intelligent of all species, the question remains: "Do we use our intelligence intelligently?" Making our lives faster and more frantic with each passing day, in my opinion, is not intelligent. But that is exactly what we are doing.

Enquiring about ourselves, our creator, and our purpose, in my opinion, is the single most effective way to use our intellectual powers. That is the primary purpose for which we have been provided with a questioning mind. We can shape our lives in the way we wish *after* acquiring this fundamental knowledge about our existence. But enquiring about spiritual truths has to be the first step. Otherwise, we would just be running aimlessly all our lives and that would be a complete waste of the rare opportunity this human life is.

The Bhagavad Gita can help you avoid making this mistake and live a meaningful life.

But why should you care to read the Bhagavad Gita and understand its philosophy if you are not a Hindu or do not believe in religion or God?

No religion or belief stops us from exploring further.

I am a Hindu by birth. But that did not stop me from reading the Bible, the Quran, the Dhammapada, and a slew of other non-Hindu scriptures.

Rather than adhering to any faith or philosophy by default, I believe in learning about different ideologies with an unbiased mind, and then adhering to the one that appeals the most to the seeker, holding utmost respect for all the other beliefs as well.

We should be open to ideas we have not heard before and accept the ones we believe have validity. The only way we can progress is by getting out of our comfort zones. That is the only way we can broaden our horizons and live more fulfilling lives.

My goal in this book is to make you aware of the philosophy that I have found to be the most enlightening one in my several years of research in the fields of spirituality and religion.

In any case, the Bhagavad Gita is *not* a religious book; rather, it teaches a very practical and logical way of living. Its philosophy and teachings can be followed by adherents of any ideology. The Bhagavad Gita (meaning "the Song of God") contains the teachings given by Lord Krishna to Prince Arjuna on the battlefield of Kurukshetra when the latter had lost his composure and forgotten his responsibilities after seeing his loved ones standing on the opposite side ready to fight him. The seven hundred and one verses of the Bhagavad Gita are believed to contain the nectar of the *Sanatana Dharma* (meaning "the Eternal Religion"), as documented in the Vedas, the oldest religious texts ever, penned by the author form of God Himself, Veda Vyasa.

In this short book, I will give you a *few* of the hundreds of reasons why you *must* consider reading the Bhagavad Gita. I will not be discussing the exact teachings of the Bhagavad Gita here; instead, my focus would be to encourage you to develop an *interest* in those teachings. This book will just touch upon a handful of the many factors that make the Bhagavad Gita unique.

This book will help you develop a strong sense of confidence in the teachings of the Bhagavad Gita. And, once you have seen what the Bhagavad Gita can do for you, the choice would be completely yours. If you believe you would like to plunge into its vast repository of divine wisdom, I will put you in the right direction. And if not, you would be free to go about your life as usual.

The reason I decided to write this book is simple: I believe time is our most valuable possession. I would not want you to go out and buy a thousand-page book on the Gita and then read it with no enthusiasm. No literature, including the Bhagavad Gita, is meant to be read by everyone. Even though it is near and dear to my heart, I would not want you to spend a second of your time on it without first determining if it is right for you.

The Bhagavad Gita, like any other philosophy, needs faith and commitment. Only if you have faith that it can help you change your life, and the commitment to understand it fully, will you be able to extract the nectar of everlasting peace and happiness it contains. Otherwise, you will just be wasting your time reading it.

Many spiritualists consider the Bhagavad Gita to be the instruction manual for human life. And I am one of them. The Bhagavad Gita contains divine teachings that, if applied, can fill one's life with endless joy.

But I do not want to give anything away in the introduction. Continue reading to learn what makes the Bhagavad Gita so special.

Important Note: At several places in this book, I would be referring to a few of the other books written by myself on the subject of the Bhagavad Gita. However, I urge you not to consider those references as 'self-promotion.' My objective in this book is to make readers aware about the magical knowledge contained in the Bhagavad Gita and direct them to what I truly believe to be the most helpful resources on the subject. And since I have put in many years of effort in writing those books, I can vouch for their accuracy and quality. However, if you have issues regarding inclusion of references to my other books herein, I request you not to read further and return this book immediately.

Chapter 1 - Is the Oldest Philosophy

"And I am seated in the hearts of all; from Me come memory, knowledge, as well as their loss; I am verily the one to be known through the study of the Vedas; indeed, I am the compiler of Vedanta, and I am the knower of the Vedas." [BG 15.15]

The hackneyed saying "old is gold" has not lost any of its meaning. And in spirituality, its relevance is even more, well, relevant.

If we assume that God is the oldest being (which would be a reasonable assumption), then His instructions must be fairly old as well.

On this note, let us look at the timeline of the birth of the world's major faiths and spiritual systems. Now, I am neither an archaeologist nor a historian. I gathered the information given below from a variety of studies and research. Also, I suggest not to consider the years mentioned here as absolute dates. They are only rough estimates of when these faiths are believed to have originated.

- Hinduism - 3000 BCE (several studies place the date as early as 6000 BCE)
- Judaism - 650 BCE

- Zoroastrianism - 600 BCE
- Buddhism - 550 BCE
- Confucianism - 550 BCE
- Jainism - 525 BCE
- Taoism - 350 BCE
- Shintoism - 300 BCE
- Stoicism - 300 BCE
- Christianity - 1 CE
- Zen - 500 CE
- Islam - 600 CE
- Sikhism - 1475 CE
- Baha'i Faith - 1850 CE

Although there are wide disagreements over the exact dates when these religions and philosophies were born, one fact that all experts agree on is that Hinduism is the world's oldest religion.

Now although I am a Hindu by birth, I am not presenting these facts to brag about 'my' religion. If I were among those who believe in mindlessly following a religion because one's parents do so, I would not have devoted the best years of my life to studying various religions when my friends were busy partying in pubs. While studying any religion, I have always maintained a completely neutral viewpoint and have treated all religions equally.

In reality, I am not a follower of *any* particular world religion. Because we are all fundamentally the same, I believe we can only have one common religion that is eternal and universal. And that religion, I discovered, is the *Sanatana Dharma* — the common religion of humankind. I have always been a seeker of truth. And the truth, in my opinion, based on decades of research, is contained in the Vedic scriptures, on which ancient Hinduism and Sanatana Dharma are based. And that is why I do my best to adhere to Vedic principles and propagate them as much as I can.

Now that we know Hinduism is the oldest religion, we should also know that the Vedas, the scriptures of Hinduism and Sanatana Dharma, are (not surprisingly) the oldest religious texts.

The Million-Year-Old Knowledge

So far, I have based the explanation only on historical data and research. Let us now go even farther in determining how old the information contained in the Bhagavad Gita really is, and see what Lord Krishna says about it in the Bhagavad Gita itself:

"I taught this imperishable Yoga (the science of getting one with God) to Vivasvan (the sun-god); Vivasvan taught it to Manu (the father of humankind); and Manu passed it on to Ikshvaku (the founder of the solar dynasty in which the

Lord appeared as Rama). This knowledge was thus handed down through orderly succession, and was received by the royal sages in that way. But, by long lapse of time here, the great science of Yoga was lost, O Parantapa. Verily, that same ancient science of Yoga is today told to you by Me, as you are My devotee as well as My friend. This knowledge is a supreme secret." [BG 4.1-4.3]

Krishna lays out the history of spiritual knowledge in these lines, leaving no room for speculation or doubt. It all makes sense, especially when we consider all the other information found in the Bhagavad Gita and the other Vedic texts. When all of this information is considered together, it becomes clear how the eternal divine knowledge has been transmitted down through the ages. Although the Bhagavad Gita was sung by Lord Krishna five thousand years ago, the knowledge contained in it was disseminated by Him as soon as He created the universe. That is why it is the purest and the most original form of knowledge.

A simple way by which we can establish the credibility of the Vedic scriptures is to measure the prophecies made in them against the evidence we have. For example, we can find the prediction about the appearance of Lord Shiva as Shankaracharya in Padma Purana. We can also find the precise prediction about the appearance of Lord Krishna as Chaitanya Mahaprabhu in several Vedic texts like Srimad Bhagavatam,

Garuda Prana, Padma Purana, Narsimha Purana, Bhavishya Purana, Vayu Purana, Narada Purana, Skanda Purana, and Matsya Purana.

It is worth noting that there is one more incarnation of Lord Krishna, who is yet to appear on earth. His name is Kalki. According to Srimad Bhagavatam, "At the end of the Kaliyuga, when there would be no Godly subjects, except in the homes of so-called sages and decent men of the higher castes, and when the power of government would be transferred to ministers elected from the lower castes, and when no one would know how to make sacrifices, the Lord will appear as the ultimate chastiser." [SB 2.7.38]

The Vedic scriptures not only predict the appearance of many manifestations of God, but they also foretell how societies and cultures would change with time. For example, it was clearly predicted that in the present age, *Kaliyuga* (or the dark age), people would lose touch with their spiritual truths and engage in sense-pleasing pursuits, seeing material pleasure as the ultimate purpose of life. And this is exactly what we see happening today.

A thorough examination of the Vedic philosophy, science, and literature, summarized by the Lord in His divine song, the Bhagavad Gita, will prove to the open-minded seeker that all truth can be found therein.

That is what Sanatana Dharma is — it has always existed, will always exist, encompasses all knowledge, and applies to everyone. This is the faith that I practice and preach. Read on to learn more.

Chapter 2 - Provides a Complete Description of God

"(I am) the goal, the maintainer, the Lord, the witness, the abode, the refuge, the dearest friend, the origin, the annihilation, the foundation, the treasure-house, and the imperishable seed." [BG 9.18]

We humans have always been curious to know if there is a Creator who has made us, and if yes, then who He is, how He looks, and where He lives. All religions describe God in their own ways. And many ideologies do not believe in the existence of God at all.

If an ideology does not believe in the existence of God (a creator and maintainer), it assumes that everything was created accidentally. However, we can clearly see the magic of God's presence all around us. Albert Einstein was so correct when he said, "The deeper one penetrates into nature's secrets, the greater becomes one's respect for God." To feel God's existence, all we need to do is to *observe* nature with an open mind free from ego and prejudice.

Let us begin by looking at our own bodies. We have eyes to see, ears to hear, a mouth to eat and communicate with, a digestion system, a respiration system, a reproduction system, and a complex arrangement of cells on our skin to cover it all. How possible is it that such a grand design was built accidentally?

Consider the millions of species of life, the billions of galaxies in space, the sun that gives us light, the moon that keeps the night sky bright, the seasons, the rains, the mountains, the rivers, grass sprouting from the soil, a baby being born, our complex brains, our ability to think and make decisions — everything, tangible or intangible, clearly pointing to one thing — that there is a power much greater than we can comprehend that keeps this whole creation running.

Is it by chance that we have oxygen, water, food, and everything else we need to survive on this planet? How could the birds, animals, fishes, and insects have been created by accident? Is it just luck that gravity holds us anchored to the ground?

There is enough evidence around us to prove without a doubt that the universe is managed by a Supreme Being. God's presence is too obvious to ignore.

Vedic literature explains in detail every fact concerning God. It reveals *everything* about Him, including how He looks, what He likes, where He lives, why He made us, and what He wants of us.

And the Bhagavad Gita summarizes all these details for our benefit.

Veda is a Sanskrit word meaning 'knowledge,' and Vedic literature contains everything worthy of being called "knowledge."

I believe in taking the finest lessons from all faiths and ideologies and applying them to my own life. However, I have discovered that Vedic literature incorporates all of those teachings in its own unique way, making it a highly comprehensive philosophy to pursue and a single source for all the answers and solutions. Whenever I learn something new about a particular philosophy, I quickly realize that it has already been handled in the Vedic texts, even though I may have never considered it that way.

I can vouch for the fact that the Vedic philosophy provides all the spiritual wisdom that we need because I live it every day. And the Bhagavad Gita summarizes that vast amount of knowledge in an easily digestible form.

Chapter 3 - Gives a Logical Description of Our True Identity

"Just as a person, casting off worn-out clothes, puts on other new ones, in the same way, the embodied (the soul), relinquishing decayed bodies, verily accepts other new ones."
[BG 2.22]

This is another factor that makes the revelations in the Bhagavad Gita special.

Let me share an extraordinary experience I had when I was nineteen.

One night as I was preparing to sleep, a strange thing happened. I heard somebody inside of me speak, and all it said was, "You are not who you think you are." I still find myself at a loss for words to describe how it felt. Yet I remember the sensation vividly. It was unlike anything I had experienced until that point in my life. For the first time, I felt like there is something more to life than what we usually consider. This was the first time I considered the presence of anything other than what my senses could perceive.

My parents had always taught me the value of worshipping God. But it was the first time I *sensed* a force much greater than my mind could comprehend — almost Godly. It was definitely not a hallucination or a dream. It was very real. I spent the night wondering what it meant — "You are not who you think you are." The more I thought about it, the more intrigued I became. For the first time in my life, I felt compelled to discover who I am, what my place in the universe is, how and why everything was created, who created everything, and what keeps the universe running. This was my first foray into the world of spirituality.

I now know what those words meant. And it is easy to guess where I might have got my answers. Yes, it was the Bhagavad Gita, our universal guide, that quenched my thirst for self-knowledge that I had carried for several years following the incident.

Most people spend their entire lives assuming they are nothing more than what they appear to be. They never question the validity of the identities that get assigned to them the moment they are born. They live under the notion that their names, families, ages, houses, neighborhoods, cities, countries, qualifications, vocations, and designations define their identities. In other words, all their lives, they identify themselves with their bodies.

And that is a huge mistake, because we are *not* our bodies.

We are not who we *think* we are.

You don't believe me? Read on.

Let us assume we are our bodies. So, when a loved one passes away, there should be no need to be sad. We can safely preserve the body in a cooling system. Will it, however, make us happy? Clearly, no. Because we do not need just the body. We need *life* within the body.

Let us look at this from a different angle. Suppose you have just learned that you have won a big reward in a lottery and are overjoyed. Now, if you and your body are the same, it implies that your body is overjoyed. But is it so? Obviously not. You may say, "My mind is overjoyed." But when you say "my body" or "my mind" you clearly imply that you are not your body or mind. This is because 'you' and 'your body' or 'you' and 'your mind' cannot be the same thing. When you say, "my body," you imply that the 'body' you are referring to is yours. Can *you* and something *you own* be the same? Clearly, no. Nothing can belong to itself.

All of this just serves to emphasize the eternal reality that WE ARE NOT OUR BODIES.

I might have just taken away the identity that you have been living with for so long. I am sorry for that, but this is something you *must* understand if you are serious about your spiritual success.

But if you are not your body or your mind, then who *are* you?

The Bhagavad Gita contains the most convincing and logical response to this age-old question. It goes into great detail about who we are, where we have come from, and how we may control our own destinies. It describes our real purpose and what can truly satisfy us.

Nobody knows more about a gadget than the company that makes it, and it describes everything about the gadget in the user manual. In the same way, nobody knows us better than our Creator. And He has described everything about us in the Bhagavad Gita, the life manual of mankind.

The Bhagavad Gita is the only spiritual and philosophical text that goes into such depth about our true nature. And this again makes the collective teachings of the Bhagavad Gita a very rational philosophy to pursue.

Chapter 4 - Describes the Purpose of Human Lives in Detail

"After numerous births, the wise man attains Me, realizing Me to be everything. Such a great soul is very hard to find."
[BG 7.19]

If nothing happens by chance and there is a Creator who plans and creates everything, it should go without saying that everything He produces has a *purpose*.

To put it another way, if God created you, you must have a certain purpose in life.

Before you go any further, be sure you understand this, since it is one of the most fundamental concepts to grasp for you to succeed spiritually.

So, your life has a purpose. But what is it exactly?

Before you can figure out your life's purpose, it is important that you understand what is *not* your life's purpose.

When I began to develop an interest in spirituality, after the transcendental experience I described in the previous chapter, I also started to feel a sense of void. I was in college, preparing for a successful career in finance and accounting, when I realized that simply having a career and spending all of one's time earning money could not be the purpose of human life. Human life could not have such a dull materialistic goal. It *had* to be something grander and divine.

Nothing changed for the next five years. By then, I had become a qualified accountant and was working for a reputed multinational accounting firm. On the spiritual front, I had already studied vast amounts of spiritual literature. And finally, the day came when I started reading the Bhagavad Gita. The outcomes were completely unexpected. It turned out to have all the answers I was looking for. Gradually, it dispelled all of my illusions and altered the course of my life.

If you are like most people, you will go to school and college to get a degree, and then work for money for most of your life. When you notice your body no longer has the strength to go on, you will retire and relax for a few days, until it's time to leave. Along the way, you will also have some fun. If you are lucky, you will also have a good family life and have a few friends to hang out with. What are the chances, according to you, that any of this is the divine purpose for which God has sent you here?

Imagine God telling you, "Go to Earth and spend your life working your heart out. Make a lot of money, have a lot of fun, and then leave it all behind and come back when your time is up."

What purpose will this serve? Nothing, if you ask me.

Yet, this is how we all spend our lives. We never pause to evaluate whether we have a life purpose and whether we are acting in ways that will help us in achieving it.

We convince ourselves that there is no such thing as a God-given life purpose. We rid ourselves of the stress of adjusting to a different way of living. We are afraid of standing out in a crowd. That is why we never give spirituality the attention it deserves.

Most of us set mundane goals for ourselves, such as making a lot of money, settling in a country or city that we love, buying a huge house, owning a dream car, marrying the boy or girl of our fantasies, retiring with a large bank balance, or even taking the last ride in a golden coffin!

Others have grander ambitions, such as discovering the cure for cancer, establishing a free hospital for the poor, winning an Olympic medal for their country, raising a child to become a doctor, and so on.

But all of these aims and ambitions, even the nobler ones, suffer from one basic flaw. Working for them is perfectly fine, but these are not enough to make one *spiritually* successful. In other words, those are not our *divine* goals.

How can they be? Can something be its own purpose? Of course, no. Will you be satisfied if you build a free hospital to help the needy, but no one shows up for treatment? The establishment of the hospital was not the real purpose you had in mind. The real purpose was to provide free treatment to the poor, which is something *external* to the establishment of the hospital.

Now, if nothing can be a purpose in and of itself, how can anything you start and finish in this life be the goal of your life? The goal of life must be something that exists outside of life, something that extends *beyond* life.

Most of us do not even consider the possibility of having a higher purpose, let alone the consequences of failing to achieve it.

Some of us believe that the purpose of life is to live morally and to help others. And some say that the goal is to keep our minds free of any negative thoughts. While it is all good to be ethical, serve others, and keep one's mind pure through meditation and mindfulness, none of these extend beyond material life.

The Vedic teachings, including the Bhagavad Gita, also encourage us to live morally and to keep our minds free of negativity. In fact, the Bhagavad Gita provides clear instructions about what constitutes good charity and good meditation. These scriptures do not, however, consider any of these to be the ultimate goal of our lives. They consider these, at best, as means to an end. As I already stated, our purpose cannot be limited to material existence. It is something a lot bigger than that.

If you want to know what your life's ultimate purpose is, I recommend studying the Bhagavad Gita. It is all laid out in great detail there, and the logic is so sound that you may be surprised you did not realize it for yourself.

Chapter 5 - Logically Explains What Happens After Death

"But never indeed, I, at any time, did not exist, nor you, nor all these rulers of men; nor verily, will any of us ever cease to exist hereafter." [BG 2.12]

Most people are fascinated by the idea of a 'life after life.' This has always been a topic of interest, not just among the seekers and spiritualists, but also among others. But again, most of us are too lazy to put in the effort to discover the truth about the existence of a 'life after life' (or 'life after death,' if you prefer).

However, since you have shown interest in reading a book about the Bhagavad Gita, you clearly have that much-needed curiosity.

The first question that needs to be answered here is: "What exactly is death?"

I know it is not the most pleasurable thing to discuss. However, refusing to talk about it does not change the fact that, like me, you will die one day. So, it is preferable to fully understand death while we are still alive. Something good may come out of it; who knows? (Spoiler: Death is all good for those who know its reality.)

So, let me ask again: What do you think death is?

When I ask this question to amateur seekers, I get a variety of responses. Here are a few examples:

"Death is the end of it all! I don't think there's any possibility of life after death."

"When a person dies, he enters a court where God judges his conduct and either rewards or punishes him."

"Depending on one's actions in this life, one goes to hell or heaven after death, and lives there for eternity."

"When a person dies, he reincarnates as a new human being on this planet."

The Bhagavad Gita provides a complete and logical explanation of death and its significance in the overall system of God for managing this universe.

The Bhagavad Gita connects our true nature, God's true nature, the purpose of our existence, death, and reincarnation in such a way that everything becomes crystal clear to a seeker who reads it with an open mind.

Different religions and ideologies have different explanations of death and reincarnation. Some believe in rebirth, and some do not. I would not spend time here to compare and contrast these different viewpoints. Instead, I would like to leave you with a few thoughts to ponder.

If you believe that death is the end of everything and that there is nothing beyond it, aren't you effectively denying the existence of God? After all, if a person only has one life and may therefore spend it in whatever way he wants (even immorally) without fear of repercussions after death, what is the need for a God? And if there is a God, and still there is nothing after death, allowing us to live unethically, then He must be a very inefficient God, which is a total impossibility.

Again, if we only have one life and our fate is decided based on our conduct in this one life as to whether we will spend eternity with God or not, how is it fair that small children die without ever having the chance to prove their worth?

Also, how can one make sure that he goes to heaven rather than hell? What method does God use to keep track of the score? Do moral acts take precedence over the development of positive mental qualities, or is it the other way around?

Where can we find the rules of the game?

I am afraid this book has enough space for the answer to just one of these questions. And I choose to answer the last one.

The Bhagavad Gita contains all the 'rules' (and all the answers), written in a very coherent manner, that makes perfect sense.

Read it and be enlightened.

Chapter 6 - Shows the Real Form of God

"O Gudakesha (Arjuna), behold in My body the entire universe together at the same place, including the moving and the non-moving, and whatever else you wish to see." [BG 11.7]

One of the most popular chapters of the Bhagavad Gita is Chapter 11, in which the Lord reveals His divine, opulent, universal, and real form.

This chapter of the Bhagavad Gita provides the vivid exposition of the actual form of God, that most seekers are always desperate to discover.

At the request of His great devotee Arjuna, Lord Krishna agrees to show him His universal form. This was a moment of glory for not only Arjuna, but for all the pure devotees of the Lord, because it was one of those very rare occasions when He revealed His true, all-encompassing form.

Sanjaya, the narrator of the Bhagavad Gita, and Arjuna, to whom the Lord sang His eternal song, were both given divine eyes, allowing them to see the mystical, beginningless, and endless form of the Almighty Lord Krishna. The magnificent epic Mahabharata mentions only one more instance when Lord Krishna displayed His divine cosmic form.

The Bhagavad Gita describes the universal form of Krishna as having numerous mouths and eyes and numerous wonderful sights, wearing numerous divine ornaments, uplifting numerous divine weapons, wearing celestial garlands and apparel, anointed with divine scents — a body all-wonderful, brilliant, unlimited, facing all sides. If thousands of suns were to shine all at once in the sky, that might equal the radiance emanating from that great soul. Arjuna could see in that form many arms, bellies, mouths and eyes, thighs and feet, and the expanded forms did not have any beginning, middle, or end. The form is described to be adorned with various crowns, clubs, and discs, with the sun and the moon as its eyes and blazing fire coming from its mouths, heating the entire universe with its radiance. This form is said to be pervading the entire universe — giving birth to everything and also annihilating everything.

I know what you might be thinking after reading this rather fearful description of the cosmic form of God — "How can God have such a horrific form? God has to be someone sober-looking and kind. He has to be someone who makes us want to look at him endlessly rather than make us scared. This depiction of God is the polar opposite of how God should look."

I get it. And I agree. And so does Krishna.

This form of the Lord is indeed terrifying. In fact, it is described in the Bhagavad Gita that after seeing this form of Krishna, Arjuna was so horrified that he requested the Lord to return to His normal two-handed form. Krishna then reverted to His initial state and told Arjuna that He knew how frightening and difficult it is for us to see and love this form of His. That is why He expects His devotees to think about Him in His blissful, Krishna-like form rather than His scary universal form.

After seeing Krishna's fantastic cosmic form, Arjuna says, "You are the primal God, the oldest person; You are the supreme refuge of this universe. You are the knower, the knowable, and the supreme abode. O being of unlimited forms, the universe is pervaded by You!" [BG 11.38]

Such are the qualities of God. And He is totally expected to possess such qualities. He is, after all, the source of *everything*. And so, it is expected that His actual form will include everything. And that is exactly how the cosmic form of Krishna is. It embraces all elements of the universe. It is also expected to be the absorber of everything, and this is exactly what Arjuna could see in that universal form — everything and everyone being sucked in.

It is very obvious that God would have a form such as this. And what I have described here is no more than a glimpse of that form as detailed in the Bhagavad Gita. The Bhagavad Gita is indeed a remarkable source of wisdom.

Chapter 7 - Clearly Distinguishes Between the Supreme God and the Demigods

"The rewards gained by men of little intelligence are limited.
The worshipers of the demigods go to the abodes of the
respective demigods; whereas, My devotees come to Me."
[BG 7.23]

Vedic literature and its holy culmination, the Bhagavad Gita, provide a *complete* picture of how God functions and manages His entire creation.

The Vedas reveal in detail how the Supreme Lord Krishna created the entire universe and the various life forms, as well as His motivations for doing so, and how He maintains His creation. And the *Devatas* (also referred to as the *Devas*) form an important part of His system. The Devatas are demigods and can be understood to be the departmental heads of God's kingdom. I devote an entire chapter to this topic in my book *30 Days to Understanding the Bhagavad Gita*.

Being born in a Hindu family, I grew up worshipping quite a lot of gods and goddesses. But I was always curious to know who the *real* God is. It never made sense to me to worship so many gods. I always felt that we were doing it all wrong. There has to be some sort of hierarchy in the spiritual world. And when I read the Bhagavad Gita, all of my confusion vanished.

The concept of demigods is rather straightforward. Krishna appoints demigods and assigns them specific departments to manage, much like a government has multiple departments that handle the different and critical responsibilities required to run a country efficiently. This might look to be an oversimplification, but there is no better way to comprehend the relationship between Krishna and the demigods.

However, Krishna did not create demigods solely for the sake of keeping the universe functioning smoothly. That is something He could do Himself. The true goal is to test the *priorities* of seekers. For example, Goddess Laksmi is worshipped by those who value wealth above Krishna's association, Goddess Saraswati is worshipped by those who prefer gaining material knowledge to Krishna's love, Lord Hanuman is worshipped by those who desire power and protection more than Krishna's blessings, and so on. However, one who has no desire for material objects and simply craves the Lord's company will only worship Krishna with a pure heart, knowing Him to be the Absolute Truth. And only such a devotee is considered a first-class devotee in Krishna's eyes deserving of His love and attention.

What the seekers who idolize the demigods do not realize is that they are merely worshiping the ministers and not the King. The Vedas affirm that worshipping Lord Krishna grants a devotee all of the benefits of worshipping all of the demigods taken together (although this should never be the motivation for worshipping Krishna).

Not realizing the distinction between God and the demigods is a major problem for adherents of all polytheistic religions and beliefs, particularly Hinduism. The majority of Hindus have no understanding of *why* they worship a specific deity. They usually choose a primary deity to worship based on two criteria. They either worship a god because it is a familial tradition to worship the same deity, or they choose a deity because they admire the deity's powers. Neither of these two grounds is logical because neither is founded on sufficient knowledge.

Religion and spirituality are important subjects that should never be taken lightly, and all decisions related to them should be taken in the light of adequate understanding. However, in this day and age, these are the very things that have taken a backseat (as was already predicted in the Vedas).

We have no interest in educating ourselves about the various philosophies and faiths and then making an unbiased and logical decision for ourselves about which one to follow. We form our beliefs based on what others believe. And those *others* believe something is true because it was believed to be true by someone else. And the chain continues. We never question our belief systems. And that is sad.

Chapter 8 - Clearly Describes the Different States of the Mind

"*Sattva* (the mode of purity), *Rajas* (the mode of passion), *Tamas* (the mode of darkness) — these *Gunas* (attributes) born of *Prakriti* (material nature) bind the imperishable, embodied one (the soul) in the body, O Mahabaho (Arjuna)."
[BG 14.5]

As you know, any feeling, emotion, thought, or idea originates in the mind. And this is what makes our minds important tools for us in our spiritual pursuits. In many ways, our spiritual quotient is decided by the qualities currently existing in our minds.

Almost all religions and faiths emphasize the importance of cultivating positive mental attributes for a spiritual seeker. These attributes include kindness, integrity, patience, courage, humility, and cheerfulness, to name a few.

They also advise seekers not to rent any space to negative emotions in their minds. Greed, anger, fear, worry, addiction, selfishness, dishonesty, and pride are the main negative emotions that most religions and philosophies urge their followers to avoid. (I will discuss more on the positive and negative traits of a seeker according to the Bhagavad Gita in Chapter 14 of this book.)

Isn't it, however, ingrained in human nature to foster positive traits while avoiding negative ones? So, what role does religion play in all of this? Don't we already know what we need to do with our minds?

The Bhagavad Gita goes a step (in fact, several steps) further. It does not simply advise us to be good, kind, and brave. It does not just teach us not to be afraid, angry, or egotistical. It goes over the ramifications of acquiring or avoiding positive or negative attributes in great depth. Now, this is something we think we understand, but actually, we don't.

According to the Bhagavad Gita, the collective mental attributes of a human being belong to one of the three modes of consciousness. These are the modes of -
1. Purity,
2. Passion, and
3. Darkness.

The Bhagavad Gita goes into great length about each of these three categories of *material* nature, including which traits belong in which, the ideal mode of consciousness to be in, and the effects of being in each mode on one's spiritual advancement.

The Bhagavad Gita's teachings, in fact, extend well beyond these three modes of material nature. If one wants to reach the Supreme Person, one must rise *above* these three modes and reach an even higher degree of consciousness. But, for transcending these modes, we need to first understand these fully and then work our way through them one by one. In the Kaliyuga, transcendental traits cannot be developed directly without first passing through the modes of material nature. This is why it is crucial for a seeker to comprehend these modes.

This is one of the most significant (yet often overlooked) concepts in the Bhagavad Gita. You can learn all about this in *30 Days to Understanding the Bhagavad Gita*, where I devote an entire chapter to this topic and go over it thoroughly.

Chapter 9 - Fully Explains All the Steps to Reach God

"They who, through the eye of knowledge, know thus the difference between the 'field' (body) and the 'knower of the field' (Supreme Soul — God), and understand the process of attaining liberation from the 'nature of the being' (material nature), reach the Supreme." [BG 13.35]

It is quite obvious that not every one of us will attain God. Neither is it that easy, nor are all of us that fortunate.

But if that is the case, there must be some qualities that one needs to possess for God to consider us for a place in His heavenly abode.

I know, I know — I have already talked about the modes of material nature. But I also said at the end of that chapter that we need to rise *above* all of those three modes (even the mode of purity) to reach Godhead.

How do we go about doing that? What is the process that we must go through to be qualified for a meeting with God, and possibly get to stay with Him forever?

Now, I will not tell you where to look for the answer. You can take a guess now.

The Bhagavad Gita is not a book full of claims about how awesome God is. Though it describes Krishna's greatness and His role as the creator of all things, recounting His magnificence is not the aim of the Bhagavad Gita.

Krishna exposes His majesty in the Bhagavad Gita for the benefit of all humankind, because we will not be able to progress spiritually unless we understand who God truly is and what His capabilities and traits are. The real aim of the Bhagavad Gita is to assist humanity in moving in the correct direction.

For this, Krishna lays down the exact steps for us to reach Him in a very straightforward and to-the-point manner. Although it may seem difficult to comprehend for a beginner, making it too simplistic would have been counterproductive, as we have a tendency to disregard anything that is easy to grasp. Complexity appeals to our intellect, especially when it comes to spirituality. A simple philosophy appears to be erroneous and fraudulent to us.

Also, if the Bhagavad Gita was spoken by Krishna in an overly simplistic manner, it would not have tested the resilience of a true seeker, and differentiated him from someone who is not willing to go the extra mile to gain true spiritual knowledge.

And if you want to understand the Bhagavad Gita in a practical and simple manner, then you can consider reading *30 Days to Understanding the Bhagavad Gita - A Complete, Simple, and Step-by-Step Guide to the Million-Year-Old Confidential Knowledge.*

The Bhagavad Gita goes far beyond giving the already-known advice to live morally and do good. It provides very practical and rational guidance on what God expects from a devotee.

For example, one of the requirements that Lord Krishna states is that one must abstain from indulging in the gratification of material senses. This makes perfect sense, as one who is overly tied to sense satisfaction will never be able to devote himself wholeheartedly to Krishna. Such a person would continually struggle to place Krishna above the things that he derives his entertainment from. With such an attitude, his consciousness will always be confined to the material world, and he will never be able to transcend the modes of material nature, and so will never be able to enter God's holy abode.

These are the kinds of virtues that a seeker needs to cultivate if he is serious about reaching God. For a pure-minded soul with a clear focus, these would be easy objectives to achieve. But for one who is excessively attached to the material world and lacks spiritual wisdom, fostering such qualities would be difficult and time-taking.

The bottom line is that a devoted spiritual seeker always gets Krishna's backing, and so nothing can stop him.

Chapter 10 - Gives a True Perspective on the Material World

"Having attained Me, the great souls, having reached the highest perfection, never take birth again in the temporary place full of miseries (the material world)." [BG 8.15]

Before you start reading this chapter, keep in mind that it will require you to have a more welcoming mind than the prior chapters. This is because I am about to denounce the very world in which we are going to spend our entire lives.

We all have our own views on the world. Most of us regard this world as a beautiful place to live. There is a lot to be happy about. There are so many different places that we can visit and so many fun activities that we can do. Technology has given us a host of new toys with which we can entertain ourselves. We can also drink, have sex, throw parties, and dance in a pub. We can watch movies and TV shows, play video games, watch and play sports, and listen to our favorite music. We have an infinite number of ways to keep ourselves happy.

But why do we need to engage in anything enjoyable in the first place? Read this question again — very slowly, one word at a time — because otherwise, it will appear to be a foolish one. Then think of an answer.

Let me give you my answer based on what I have learned from reading the Bhagavad Gita. The only reason we need these objects of pleasure and spend time 'having fun' is that this material life is *not* fun in general. Is dragging yourself home after banging your head for twelve hours at work and watching television for an hour before sinking into bed fun? But, regardless of what we do for a livelihood or the tale our bank accounts tell, this is how most of us live. Then there are money issues, health issues, relationship issues, emotional issues, and many other issues that this book does not have space to mention. In this world, practically everyone drags their feet through life. Because admitting the reality is difficult, we consider our lives to be full of fun. Optimism feels great, but it does little to get us out of the mess.

Self-help and motivational gurus do their best to propagate the idea that this world is wonderful, and we need to see it as a fantastic place to enjoy no matter what situation we are in. They are obviously expected to say such things as this is their business — to show people a dream world where everything is great. Imagine a motivational speaker declaring that the world is full of suffering, and it is not possible to find any real happiness here. Their business will crumble immediately. After all, their business is built on the idea of optimism. Hope is the product they sell. It does not matter to them whether the product bears any truth or not. It sells anyway, as these gurus make people believe they have a solution. But actually, they don't. Anyone who has a different view of the world is considered pessimistic. Nobody wants to listen to one who speaks of pain. People love people who are upbeat and paint a rosy picture of the future.

There is nothing wrong with liking people who say positive things. However, the problem lies in the definition of the word "positive." Being positive does not imply ignoring reality and living in a fantasy world of hope. Being positive is not indulging in hours of entertainment in the hope of ridding oneself of pain. Being positive is accepting the truth and seeing things *as they are* rather than how one wishes, and then doing everything possible to improve the situation.

That is why the Bhagavad Gita is the most uplifting and inspiring book ever written. It does not paint a misleading picture of this world with everything looking perfect. Instead, it contrasts living in a materially motivated atmosphere with living in a spiritually pure environment, and allows the seeker to choose between the two.

And what if there is a much more beautiful and blissful world out there, and we are busy struggling to find artificial ways to please ourselves with material toys, disregarding it entirely? If there is a God somewhere, He must be having a home, and that home must obviously be all-blissful. Then what is the reason we do not even consider getting there? Because temporary material pleasures blind us and prevent us from looking beyond. They just do not allow us to consider what is best for us.

The Vedic scriptures describe God's abode, and we can see it is full of pure joy and free from all material contamination and negativity. It is just the way God's home is expected to be. Upon reading about it, an open-minded seeker will realize that it is not a fictional world but is very real. And it is waiting for us to arrive. It is our choice if we want to go there or are happy to confine ourselves to trivial earthly pleasures.

The Bhagavad Gita shows the way to everlasting happiness, but only after describing the truth about happiness and distress and the real reason behind their occurrence. It starts by clearing the dust, allowing a seeker to see things as they are. And then it allows him to choose the direction he would want to move in.

This is true positivity. This is true motivation. The future can indeed be bright and blissful. But for that, you will need to see and accept reality. Doing this will surely open up the doors to possibilities and happiness for you.

Chapter 11 - Explains the Role of Work in Spiritual Advancement

"Your right is indeed to perform dutiful actions, but not to the rewards. Never consider yourself as the creator of the rewards of actions, and there must never be an attachment to inaction." [BG 2.47]

In our day-to-day lives, we all do some kind of work. And I am not talking about only our professional duties here. Work includes anything we do as part of our duties, from a student studying for a test or a homemaker cooking a meal to something more complex like an astronaut learning to survive on a different planet or a doctor operating on a victim of a serious accident.

In the olden days, however, one's responsibilities were decided by the cultural rules. According to the Vedas, society was split into four classes in ancient times. These were Brahmins, Kshatriyas, Vaishyas, and Shudras.

Brahmins were society's religious leaders. Kshatriyas ruled and managed the state and protected its people from enemies and other threats. Vaishyas were merchants and farmers. And Shudras were the laborers that served the other classes.

Individuals in each of these classes had to adhere to their assigned responsibilities. For example, Arjuna, the prince to whom Lord Krishna sang the Bhagavad Gita, was a Kshatriya. When he saw his loved ones standing on the opposite side in the great war of Mahabharata, he lost his composure out of compassion for them and refused to fight. However, a Kshatriya's mandated duty was to fight for righteousness, and a Kshatriya with integrity could not refuse to fight in a battle, even if it meant inevitable death. Since Arjuna was perplexed and had forgotten his duty, Lord Krishna sang His eternal divine song to him to educate him about spiritual truths and thus help him regain his calm and sobriety.

Lord Krishna clarifies in the Bhagavad Gita that spiritual advancement is only possible for those who religiously engage in their prescribed duties. Avoiding one's responsibilities is a surefire way to spiritual degeneration. Renunciation is recommended only for fully realized souls, not seekers.

So, it is clear that one should do his best to fulfill one's responsibilities. Even though our society is no longer divided into any such classes, we all have our chosen responsibilities to fulfill. And we need to make sure we perform them to the best of our abilities.

But just working is not enough. The work should be done in the mode of purity. And what makes the work pure is the *aim* with which the work is done.

Now I know it may look terribly confusing. What else can possibly be the aim of work than the direct and indirect desired results of one's actions?

A student studies to clear his exams, a doctor works to treat his patients and earn fees in return, an employee works for his paycheck, a businessman works for profits, a homemaker works to keep the household running smoothly, and so on. Everybody works with a result in mind.

There is one thing that all success-coaches have in common. They all tell their followers to set clear, time-bound goals for themselves, and then work their tails off to achieve those goals.

But here comes the Bhagavad Gita twist. Lord Krishna instructs that one should never be concerned about the material outcome of one's endeavors. In a way, He tosses supposedly the best self-help advice ever out of the window.

Now, before you jump to any conclusions, let me inform you that this is the most misunderstood principle in the Bhagavad Gita.

How can someone work without a goal in mind? How can one be able to give it his all if he works without thinking about achieving a specific result? He will surely fail in his endeavors. Should an employee continue to work relentlessly without expecting to be paid for his efforts? Should not a student expect good grades and work toward that goal? Krishna's advice seems totally impractical and illogical.

Of course, this would seem to be absurd to anybody who just reads a verse or two of the Bhagavad Gita without inferring the complete meaning of this principle in proper context.

This concept, if grasped properly, can be life-changing. This is one of the best recipes for success ever — both materially and spiritually. This principle has the power to entirely transform one's attitude toward work and enable him to achieve whatever he desires.

All that is needed is to understand this delicate concept in a proper light.

Chapter 12 - Puts God First

"Those whose intelligence is immersed in That (the Supreme God), soul is one with That, faith is given to That, who have taken That as the supreme goal, their sins being cleansed through knowledge, reach the state of no return (liberation)."
[BG 5.17]

Most people agree that we should devote ourselves to God. But how many of us actually do that?

Standing in front of God's idol and praying to Him to grant all your wishes is not devotion; it is business. Reciting hymns from scriptures while fretting about how you will get through your huge to-do list for the day is not devotion either; it is a terrible example of multitasking.

Pure devotion includes giving your one hundred percent attention to God. And devotion is not just about prayers. Your entire life — every second of it — should be devoted to God.

Of course, you can't be thinking of God all the time. That would be foolish and is not expected at all. So don't think of God while driving a car, or you may soon find yourself standing before Him.

What is needed is that you design your life in such a way that all your activities and intentions are dedicated to God. And you should do it out of genuine love for Him.

Love for God is the highest form of emotion in the entire creation. And you should strive to reach a point when that emotion dominates your entire being.

If you are looking to live the most perfect and authentic life possible, then let me tell you that this is the highest level of perfection a human being can possibly achieve. If you are madly in love with God, and your love is pure and free of material wants, you will undoubtedly reach Him.

However, many spiritualists believe that the best human is one who serves humanity unconditionally. And they have a seemingly sound argument to support this. They argue that because we are all God's children, and because a parent loves his child more than himself, any act done to aid his child will satisfy God more than anything done to please Him directly.

If one looks at this reasoning superficially, one would conclude that it is logically valid, and that if one wishes to please God, he should engage himself in humanitarian service. The Bhagavad Gita, as well as all other Vedic scriptures, strongly advocate social service and other philanthropic efforts. They do not, however, support doing so in order to please God. The Bhagavad Gita even defines pure charity. In the Vedic philosophy, charity has a specific position. However, it should never be used as a substitute for devotion to God. As always, the Bhagavad Gita leaves nothing to guesswork and presents logical arguments to support this, thwarting all doubts one may have.

The Bhagavad Gita describes four types of progressive yogic practices, which might be thought of as four steps toward perfection and Krishna. Those are:

1. Jnana Yoga (the path of knowledge)
2. Raja Yoga (the path of meditation)
3. Karma Yoga (the path of action)
4. Bhakti Yoga (the path of devotion)

As you can see, the path of devotion is the last stage of *Yoga* (the practice aimed at uniting oneself with the Supreme). The next stage is Krishna.

Pure devotion is prioritizing Krishna over *everything* else. And "everything" includes, well, everything. That is the test of one's devotion. If reaching God is your ultimate goal, devotion to Him has to be your highest priority. No other religious text stresses this important point as much as the Bhagavad Gita.

And what exactly is devotion? You know where to look   for   the   answer.

Chapter 13 - Provides the Perfect Remedy for All Negative Emotions

"Let man lift his self (the mind) by the self (the knowledge of being a soul), not degrade his self; for the self (the mind) is the friend of oneself, and it is also the enemy." [BG 6.5]

Allow me to ask you another simple question. Do you think a person may advance spiritually if his mind is filled with negative emotions like lust, fear, worry, anger, ego, greed, or envy?

The obvious answer is "No."

A person with a lustful mind never chooses devotion to God over his material cravings. When given a choice, he chooses to satisfy his impure desires rather than to chant God's names or meditate on him with a pure mind.

A person who is scared or worried is never able to concentrate on devotion. He always expects inauspicious things to happen, and his mind is constantly occupied with finding a way out.

Ego is one of the biggest impediments to spiritual advancement. Ego does not let one see reality. It keeps one in a mental dreamland where he is the king who sets the rules. A person suffering from an egoistic mind fails to see how insignificant his position is in the grand scheme of things. All his efforts are aimed at appeasing his ego. Such a person is incapable of devotion to God.

A short-tempered person has a large ego that he must maintain. How could such a person be able to persuade his egoistic mind to give up control to someone else, even if that someone else is the all-powerful God?

Envious people are also slaves to their egos; else, they would never be jealous of what others have. When an envious person sees someone else having something he does not have, it hurts his ego. That 'something' can be something intangible, like words of appreciation from the boss, or something tangible like a bigger car.

Greed is a sign that the person suffering from it places an excessive amount of value on objects of sensory pleasure. He is never satisfied with what he has and always wants more. Such a person cannot engage in genuine spirituality, since his mind is constantly craving more material pleasure.

All of these negative emotions stem from the same source, have the same effect, and have the same solution.

The source is unconsciousness, which is nothing but a lack of awareness of one's true identity.

The effect is spiritual degradation.

The solution is divine knowledge, which leads to a comprehensive understanding of oneself and God, as well as a clear idea of one's ultimate goal in life.

People who suffer from mental disorders such as excessive fear, anger, worry, lust, ego, or envy are too immature for spirituality. They are not in the proper state of mind to pursue the path to enlightenment.

But hold on a second. Isn't it the role of spirituality to help a seeker become psychologically strong and positive?

Well, yes and no. It appears to be a chicken-and-egg situation, but actually, it is not.

This is how it works: A person suffering from one or more of these mental impurities needs to develop maturity and willingness, by himself, to get rid of these feelings permanently through spirituality. This is *our* job — mine and yours. Once one becomes willing, spirituality steps in and helps one progress further. Spirituality is only meant for one who is *willing* to grow.

When a person is ready to make spiritual (and mental) progress, spirituality (God, or Krishna) takes his hand and leads him to the solution. And the Bhagavad Gita has that solution that can rid one of all negative emotions for good. And it works all the time. It has to. It comes from Krishna.

When one bathes in the holy knowledge revealed in the Bhagavad Gita, all these impurities are washed away. His mind becomes free of stress, anxiety, fear, rage, ego, envy, lust, and any other negative feeling that has kept him from living a happy life thus far.

Such is the power of Krishna's divine song.

Chapter 14 - Describes the True Nature of a Transcendentalist

"Therefore, the scriptures are your guide in determining what should be done and what should not be done. You should act here knowing the regulations declared in the scriptures." [BG 16.24]

When I was preparing to become a professional accountant, I had to study hard to master the nitty-gritty of the laws of accounting. At the same time, I had to go through a three-and-a-half-year practical training program under the supervision of a professional accountant, during which I learned the thought process required for success in this field.

To succeed in any career, one must acquire the necessary skills and knowledge. But acquiring knowledge is not enough. One also needs to cultivate a suitable mindset — a way of thinking.

This is also relevant in the context of spirituality. To be a successful transcendentalist or seeker, one must expand his mind both intellectually and emotionally. It is impossible to achieve one's spiritual goals without cultivating a mindset suitable for enlightenment.

So how does one go about doing this?

When Arjuna regains his composure and is able to think sensibly again after gaining transcendental knowledge from Krishna, Krishna educates him about the various attributes of one who is of a divine nature and one who has a demonic nature. Knowing these characteristics can help you tell the difference between a spiritually successful person and a spiritual failure.

Most of these pure and impure attributes are quite obvious ones. For example, purity of heart, compassion, and truthfulness are all desirable attributes for a seeker, whereas dishonesty, selfishness, and wrath are not.

In *30 Days to Understanding the Bhagavad Gita*, I list down more than twenty-five desirable and more than twenty undesirable traits that a seeker should develop and avoid respectively, as revealed by Lord Krishna in the Bhagavad Gita.

Having a list like this handy is quite useful. It acts as a compass for us as we strive to achieve perfect consciousness. It prevents us from falling down and keeps us on the right path. This again makes the Bhagavad Gita a very practical and seeker-friendly spiritual text. There is nothing vague about it. Also, it does not speak at a level that only a few can comprehend, but rather in a way that we all can understand.

But just going through the list is obviously not sufficient. Having the determination to tread that path is what matters, especially in *Kaliyuga* — the age we are living in. Today, it is common to lie to someone for one's own benefit. Compassion is a rare trait. Anger has become the normal state of mind. It is difficult to cultivate even one of these attributes fully, let alone the other twenty-five or so. Today, ego rules our minds. Lust dictates our behavior. Very few are interested in gaining true knowledge. Staying away from so many undesirable traits looks completely impossible.

But nothing is impossible for one with a resolute mind. Help from Krishna is readily available for such a devotee. With His aid, countless seekers have been able to transcend the afflictions of this mortal world. God is the source of power for a sincere seeker. He is the only true treasure.

And He has given us the key to that treasure in the form of the Bhagavad Gita, a practical guide to living a perfect life and achieving our spiritual goals. If absorbed as is, without personal agendas or prejudice, the wisdom contained in the pages of this holy scripture has the potential to free you from all sorrows and sufferings and to fill your life (and afterlife) with peace and bliss. This treasure can be yours to enjoy, but only if you understand its worth and are prepared to learn more about it.

Chapter 15 - Is the Most Scientific Philosophy

"To you, who does not carp, I shall now impart this most confidential knowledge and realization, knowing which you shall be liberated from evil." [BG 9.1]

When I first became curious to know who I was (after the "You are not who you think you are" incident), and was still considering studying religion and spirituality, I had my doubts about the authenticity of the scriptures. What if the information I was considering learning did not come from authoritative sources? What if they were all lies, and I end up ruining my life because of them?

These doubts kept me awake at night. But I did not know of any way I could relieve myself of my curiosity about the eternal truths other than to read scriptures and learn about various ideologies. So, I chose to give them a shot.

I knew it would take me several years (possibly decades) to study all the major philosophies and religions in depth. But I was adamant. There was no other way for me. I just *had* to do this.

So, I persisted and continued my research. And I am happy I didn't get scared or quit in the middle. I eventually made it through this phase and gained the one thing I had always craved — the truth. When I read the Bhagavad Gita, I knew I had got there. I was certain that I had discovered the truth about myself and God. I was sure I knew my purpose in life. And I am still sure.

I have an immense amount of respect and admiration for all philosophies and religions, as I have learned a lot from each of them. But what gives me such confidence in the Vedic wisdom being the ultimate knowledge is that, according to me, it has a complete and rational framework.

There is no way for us to travel back in time and see what happened when God created the universe, this world, and life. However, we can make use of the resources that have been provided to us. That is exactly what I did. And I am so glad I did it, because I do not have to rely on guessing anymore, and I do not have to follow a philosophy in life that I am not even sure is true. I now follow what I believe to be the most scientific and rational philosophy and base my life on it, knowing that I am living the way God wants me to live.

Let me outline a few of the hundreds of reasons (some of which have already been discussed in previous chapters) why I believe Vedic knowledge, including the Bhagavad Gita, is the most scientific of all knowledge:

1. It reveals everything there is to know about God, including His abilities, forms, abode, traits, and desires.
2. It describes God as all-attractive and all-blissful — qualities that God is expected to possess.
3. It provides comprehensive spiritual information about us.
4. It teaches us everything we need to know about our lives' purpose and how to fulfill it.
5. It explains the relevance of the other forms of life.
6. It teaches us how to make decisions about our future lives.
7. It provides complete information about what happens after a living being dies.
8. The Vedic description of the entire cosmic creation is scientific and logical.
9. It offers a scientific explanation of reincarnation.
10. It puts logical emphasis on the significance of the mind as the most important tool for spiritual advancement.
11. It explains God's mechanisms for operating the entire universe.
12. It explains the various eras of humanity and the entire cycle of evolution and destruction.

13. It provides a scientific explanation of space and time, forever altering a seeker's perspective on these concepts.
14. It aids the development of spiritual interests in people who have a worldly outlook on life.
15. It explains the purpose with which God created everything.
16. It does not limit its teachings to the material realm. On the contrary, it is primarily concerned with the spiritual realm.
17. It provides a comprehensive description of the desirable and undesirable attributes of a true seeker.
18. It describes the various methods and steps to approach God.
19. It provides permanent and practical remedies to all negative and painful situations.
20. It logically explains the futility of all negative emotions.
21. It emphasizes the need for one to rise above sense gratification, as an attachment to material nature is clearly one of the most significant hurdles on the path to God.
22. It logically regards ego as another big impediment to spirituality, because a self-centered person can never embrace God's authority.

23. It logically regards unconditional devotion to God as the pinnacle of perfection.
24. It perfectly describes why we cannot see God, as well as how we can see Him.
25. It explains how to direct our work in such a way that it aids us in achieving spiritual perfection.
26. It is the oldest form of knowledge.

This is by no means an exhaustive list of reasons why you must consider acquiring Vedic knowledge. However, if you are serious about increasing your spiritual quotient, this should be enough motivation for you.

Read It to Know It

Lord Krishna declares to Arjuna in the Bhagavad Gita, "And he who will study this sacred conversation of ours, I shall have been worshipped by him (through this study) by the sacrifice of gaining knowledge; such is My opinion." [BG 18.70]

And of the doubters, He says, "However, one who is ignorant and faithless, and has a doubting mind perishes. For a person of doubting mind, there is neither this world, nor the next, nor bliss." [BG 4.40]

Spiritual knowledge is impossible to grasp for one whose mind is saturated with ego and material desires. No matter how clear things are, *Maya* — the material form of energy, will keep him from breaking free from delusion. Such souls are the most unfortunate. Our time is limited, and our end (in the present form) is near. We need to educate and then liberate ourselves as quickly as possible. No amount of money, power, and fame will save us when we cease to belong to this planet. Remember that many people have held the title of "world's richest person" in the past, and many more will do so in the future. But they all end up in the same place as the street beggar.

So, I urge you to devote some of your time to spirituality. Trust me; it is crucial.

Krishna has already helped us by condensing the enormous amount of information dispersed across several scriptures into just seven hundred and one verses. If you want an authentic and accurate translation of the Bhagavad Gita into English, you can grab the one translated by me.

And if that too looks complicated, I break down all that knowledge for you into a 30-day comprehensive program in my book *30 Days to Understanding the Bhagavad Gita*. I have written it in a very easy-to-understand style so that beginners can derive as much benefit from reading it as advanced seekers. I have included an excerpt of the introduction to that book at the end of this book so you can decide whether reading it is worth your time.

This book contained a very brief introduction to the Bhagavad Gita and the Vedic philosophy. If you found something contradictory or did not understand a concept, rest assured it is taken care of in *30 Days to Understanding the Bhagavad Gita* and other books where I had space for detailed discussions.

If this book has piqued your interest, even slightly, to learn more about the divine knowledge poured into the Bhagavad Gita by Lord Krishna, then I would highly encourage you to consider reading its translation or *30 Days to Understanding the Bhagavad Gita*. And if not, that is perfectly fine as well (thanks a ton for completing this book even when its content did not appeal to you).

Finally, I would like to express my gratitude for taking a chance on this book. Even if you got it for free (the ebook version), you still invested your time, which I consider a much bigger investment.

I wish you lots of luck in your material and spiritual endeavors and pray that you live your most authentic life.

God bless!

About the Author

Hari Chetan is a spiritual and consciousness coach and has an immense amount of experience in the fields of religion, spirituality, theology, and ancient and modern philosophy. He is an expert in all major religions and spiritual philosophies including Christianity, Hinduism, Islam, Buddhism, Sikhism, Jainism, Judaism, Stoicism, Zen, Taoism, and Baha'i. However, Vedic philosophy is his primary area of interest.

Having discovered the oldest and the most confidential spiritual wisdom contained in the Vedic scriptures, Hari is on a mission to spread this knowledge to all corners of the globe. His goal is to awaken the entire world to the true identity of the self and God, and make everyone aware of the purpose of their existence, as this is the only lasting solution to all our problems. He currently lives in Kolkata, India with his family.

Connect with Hari Chetan:

harichetan.com
hari@harichetan.com
facebook.com/HariChetanOfficial
patreon.com/HariChetan

The Bhagavad Gita Series

Book 1: Bhagavad Gita - The Perfect Philosophy: 15 Reasons That Make the Song of God the Most Scientific Ideology

Book 2: Bhagavad Gita (in English): The Authentic English Translation for Accurate and Unbiased Understanding

Book 3: 30 Days to Understanding the Bhagavad Gita: A Complete, Simple, and Step-by-Step Guide to the Million-Year-Old Confidential Knowledge

Book 4: The Bhagavad Gita Summarized and Simplified: A Comprehensive and Easy-to-Read Summary of the Divine Song of God

Book 5: Mind Management through the Bhagavad Gita: Master your Mindset in 21 Days and Discover Unlimited Happiness and Success

All Books: Bhagavad Gita (In English) – The Complete Collection: 5-Books-in-1

Introduction to
30 Days to Understanding the Bhagavad Gita
(an excerpt)

What is the Bhagavad Gita?

I'll give you a quick answer now, and the rest will be revealed over the next thirty days as you work your way through the chapters.

The Bhagavad Gita is the comprehensive instruction manual provided by God to us for living a perfect life in this material world.

The Bhagavad Gita (meaning "the Song of God") is the oldest and the most authoritative source of wisdom in the universe. I have given this topic its own chapter in this book. But for the time being, keep in mind that the information you are about to receive is not some made-up New Age nonsense. It is divine, original, and unadulterated. Lord Krishna imparted this knowledge for the first time millions of years ago, when He created the universe. And He repeated it five thousand years ago for the benefit of those who would live in the present era (more on this on Day 25).

The Bhagavad Gita is a collection of all the wisdom contained in the Vedas, the divine literature, that we need to have to fulfill our life's purpose. The Bhagavad Gita has seven hundred verses separated into eighteen chapters in which Lord Krishna explains our true identity and the sole purpose of our lives. He also reveals why He is the God, what His virtues are, and what His true form is. In short, the Bhagavad Gita provides all the knowledge that a seeker of truth may require. Understanding it leads to wisdom. Acting on it leads to freedom.

I am not going to go into detail about the magnificence of the Bhagavad Gita here, since the only way to understand it is to experience it. And this book is designed to provide you with that experience.

The purpose of this book

There are a variety of books about the Bhagavad Gita that we can read. In my own quest for spiritual wisdom, I read over a hundred books on this subject. But the biggest issue I discovered was that there was a significant lack of a step-by-step learning structure for the students of this great spiritual guide. I realized, because of the lack of a proper handbook, students became confused and found it difficult to integrate the different concepts presented in the Bhagavad Gita.

Most books about the Bhagavad Gita presented a verse-by-verse commentary. Reading the Bhagavad Gita this way can be challenging for a beginner. In my opinion, only an experienced seeker with a thorough understanding of the true spirit of the Bhagavad Gita should attempt this.

I also noticed that practically every book about the Bhagavad Gita, whether it was a verse-by-verse commentary or an explanation of its teachings, was written in a difficult-to-understand language. A book written in a simpler style that appealed to readers at all levels of consciousness was needed.

So, I decided to fill these gaps myself. And the result is in your hands.

This book is designed to assist you, no matter where you are in your spiritual journey. It covers all of the information found in the Bhagavad Gita in a way that makes it easier to understand and remember. If you are a beginner, this book will undoubtedly help you in avoiding any confusion that may occur when reading the Bhagavad Gita verse by verse. I've kept the book relatively short, keeping in mind how busy most of us are in today's world. You will learn something new every day, and it will all add up to create the desired knowledge base, which will be both complete and powerful.

Printed in Great Britain
by Amazon

25693521R00057